FEELINGS

Surprise

Tamra B. Orr

Published in the United States of America
by Cherry Lake Publishing
Ann Arbor, Michigan
www.cherrylakepublishing.com

Reading Adviser: Marla Conn MS, Ed., Literacy specialist, Read-Ability, Inc.

Photo Credits: © AJP/Shutterstock Images, cover, 1; © Andy Dean
Photography/Shutterstock Images, 4; © De Visu/Shutterstock Images, 6; ©
Monkey Business Images/Shutterstock Images, 8, 16; © wavebreakmedia/
Shutterstock Images, 10, 18; © Pressmaster/Shutterstock Images, 12; ©Tom
Wang/Shutterstock Images, 14; © Blend Images/Shutterstock Images, 20

Library of Congress Cataloging-in-Publication Data
Names: Orr, Tamra, author.
    Title: Surprise / Tamra B. Orr.
Description: Ann Arbor : Cherry Lake Pub, 2016. | Series: Feelings |
Audience: K to Grade 3. | Includes bibliographical references and index.
Identifiers: LCCN 2015048119| ISBN 9781634710480 (hardcover) | ISBN
9781634711470 (pdf) | ISBN 9781634712460 (pbk.) | ISBN 9781634713450
(ebook)
Subjects: LCSH: Surprise—Juvenile literature.
Classification: LCC BF575.S8 O77 2016 | DDC 152.4—dc23
LC record available at http://lccn.loc.gov/2015048119

Cherry Lake Publishing would like to acknowledge the work of The Partnership
for 21st Century Learning. Please visit www.p21.org for more information.

Printed in the United States of America
Corporate Graphics

Table of Contents

Shhh! It's a Secret

Today is my dad's birthday.

What do you think this girl is telling her sister?

We are having a **party**. Shhh!

It's a **surprise** party. Dad does not know about it.

It will be so fun!

Balloons and Cake

Many people come to our house. We are ready to hide.

We have **balloons**. We have a cake.

Dad will be home soon.
I cannot wait to see his face!

Happy Birthday, Dad!

Everybody hides. The lights are out. Shhh!

Dad walks in. Everyone yells, "Surprise!"

How can you tell this dad is surprised?

He jumps a little. His eyes get big.

Then he begins to laugh.

A Surprise for Everyone

Dad loves his party.
Now it is time for cake.

Mom opens the box. Inside is a **wedding** cake!

Oops! The bakery gave us the wrong cake!

How is this family feeling?

"Surprise!" says Dad.

Now we are all laughing.

Find Out More

Chaud, Benjamin. *The Bear's Surprise*. San Francisco: Chronicle Books, 2015.

Horacek, Petr. *A Surprise for Tiny Mouse*. Somerville, MA: Candlewick, 2015.

Reagan, Jean. *How to Surprise a Dad*. New York: Alfred A. Knopf, 2015.

Glossary

balloons (buh-LOONZ) air-filled plastic bags
party (PAHR-tee) people getting together to have fun
surprise (sur-PRIZE) a feeling of excitement and wonder
wedding (WED-ing) an event where two people get married

Home and School Connection

Use this list of words from the book to help your child become a better reader. Word games and writing activities can help beginning readers reinforce literacy skills.

about	everyone	know	says
all	eyes	laugh	see
are	face	lights	soon
bakery	for	little	surprise
balloons	fun	loves	the
begins	gave	many	then
big	get	mom	time
birthday	have	not	today
box	having	now	wait
cake	hide	opens	walks
cannot	his	our	wedding
come	home	out	will
dad	house	party	wrong
does	inside	people	yells
everybody	jumps	ready	

Index

About the Author

Tamra Orr has written more than 400 books for young people. The only thing she loves more than writing books is reading them. She lives in beautiful Portland, Oregon, with her husband, four children, dog, and cat. She says that her children still manage to surprise her every day.